ENGLAND
A PICTURE MEMORY

Text
Bill Harris

Captions
Fleur Robertson

Design
Teddy Hartshorn

Photography
Colour Library Books Ltd
The Telegraph Colour Library

Commissioning Editor
Andrew Preston

Publishing Assistant
Edward Doling

Editorial
Gill Waugh

Production
Ruth Arthur
Sally Connolly
David Proffit
Andrew Whitelaw

Director of Production
Gerald Hughes

Director of Publishing
David Gibbon

CLB 2523
© 1991 Colour Library Books Ltd, Godalming, Surrey, England.
All rights reserved.
This 1991 edition published by Crescent Books,
distributed by Outlet Book Company, Inc, a Random House Company,
225 Park Avenue South, New York, New York 10003.
Color reproduction by Scantrans Pte Ltd, Singapore.
Printed and bound in Hong Kong.
ISBN 0 517 05317 9
8 7 6 5 4 3 2 1

ENGLAND
A PICTURE MEMORY

CRESCENT BOOKS
NEW YORK

First page: Bickleigh village, Devon, and (previous pages) rural Derbyshire. Facing page: the Pantiles, a row of shops that has changed little in two hundred years, in Royal Tunbridge Wells, Kent.

Since the time, as the song says, "When Britain first at heaven's command arose from out the azure main," she has produced more than her fair share of heroes. Possibly the most honored is Admiral Horatio Nelson, who saved his country from Napoleon's navy. But of all the memorials to the Battle of Trafalgar, the most typically British are unmarked and unnoticed. Lord Nelson's second-in-command that day was Vice-Admiral Cuthbert Collingwood who, unlike the hero of the day, lived to enjoy a long retirement. His greatest pleasures during those years were long walks in the country, and he never walked anywhere without a pocketful of acorns, which he dropped along the way to replace the oak trees had been felled to build the British fleet.

The image of a retired admiral named Cuthbert planting trees along public footpaths is, for many of us, the picture of England itself. But it is only a snapshot of the culture that gave us William Shakespeare and Peter Rabbit, Edward Elgar and the Beatles, the Royal Family and the House of Commons. It's a culture so distinct that even Englishmen themselves often forget that they aren't a pure breed, but the product of a melting pot. During the years of Roman occupation, which lasted almost five centuries, camp-followers from every corner of the world added their genes to a mix that also includes the blood of Saxons and Celts, Normans and Danes. In spite of this, as Ogden Nash pointed out, "To be an Englishman is to belong to the most exclusive club there is."

The fact that they live on an island has something to do with it. The English Channel may not seem like much of a barrier; people have been swimming across it for years. But it's barrier enough to have kept England's neighbors in their place for more than nine-hundred years, more than enough time for the English to have developed a sense of, for lack of a better word, insularity. And now that it's beginning to look like the French and others are going to be able to invade Britain through a tunnel under the Channel, many are beginning to man the ramparts. They'll welcome the outsiders as visitors, of course, but many say they'll never surrender. When construction began, one tunnel opponent proudly claimed that he had never been to Europe and had no intentions of ever going there. When it was pointed out that England was, in fact, a part of Europe, he shot back an "are you daft?" look and dismissed the idea as an accident of geography.

Geography may also have something to do with the English passion for liberty. Throughout most of its history, England has been covered with forests and marshes that could provide food and shelter for any man with the courage to get out from under the bondage of the landowners. Such a life was hard as any life on the American frontier, but the freedom it gave made it all worthwhile. As late as the seventeenth century, more than half the land in England was wilderness, sheltering exiled nobility such as the likes of Robin Hood, as well as fugitive outlaws and men whose independent nature was fed by the forest; under greenwood, as they say. The trees began to disappear in the 1600s, not to create farmland but to build the ships that would expand England's frontiers to other parts of the world.

When the English went abroad, they took England with them, very much like the Israelites, who carried their tablets of law wherever they wandered. Over the centuries when what Ogden Nash would see as an exclusive club was developing, the English had become something very much like a family. Like every family, they had their black sheep, but they also had a spirit of compromise among themselves that makes a difference in any family and made all the difference in the British success story. Tradition may be important to the average Englishman and many don't mind telling you that theirs are best, but their traditions are far from being etched in stone. On the other hand, if you should get the notion to try changing them, be warned that it's not for nothing they're called John Bull. They won't give up without a fight.

The American tradition holds that they gave up after the fight in '76. But that disagreement was probably more a breakdown of the spirit of compromise than anything else. What the colonists wanted was the rights of Englishmen because they were, after all, Englishmen themselves. After they won their fight, they went right on speaking the English language, reading the King James Bible, operating under laws common in England and building their houses and towns in styles fashionable across the water. Their cities were still named for places in England, like Boston, Norfolk, Portsmouth and York, though we can only speculate whether they would have retained them if their predecessors had imported such names as Mousehole or Batty Moss, Higher Force or Lower Slaughter.

American visitors in England find that the language isn't quite the same. They have trouble getting used to the idea that motorcars come equipped with bonnets and boots, that a subway won't get you anywhere but across the street and that getting into the underground is often made easier with a lift. Most Americans already know that a bobby is a cop, but they don't always understand that a bob is a shilling and a copper a penny. They find that football is something quite different from the bone crushings and endless time-outs they watch at home on Monday nights, and when they get homesick for an afternoon of baseball, they don't find it at a cricket match.

Cricket and baseball claim to be the respective national pastimes of England and America. Both are said to emulate the rules of life itself and both are played on fields of bright green grass on summer afternoons. But except for the fact that the object of each game is to hit a ball with a bat, cricket is as incomprehensible to an American baseball fan as Gaelic names are to a Gaelic speaker when they are pronounced the way they are spelled.

In cricket, the pitcher is called a bowler and unlike his American counterpart, he doesn't stand on a little artificial hill in the middle of the field tugging at his cap, spitting tobacco juice and contorting his body as though he has an itch he can't quite reach. This athlete bounds onto the field like a spring lamb and with a stiff-armed pitch hurls a ball toward a batsman who is guarding three upright sticks called a wicket. There is another wicket twenty-two yards away guarded by a second batsman who, like his teammate, is armed with a long flat paddle designed to slam the ball away from the wicket. If one of them hits the speeding red ball, he doesn't instinctively toss away the bat and start running as his American counterparts do. He gives his next action a bit of thought. If it looks like one of the opposing team's fielders might quickly return the ball, he can stand pat and remain safe. But if he decides to run, the other batsman has to run, too. Each of them is required to get to the other wicket, to touch a mark on it with his bat and then get back to his original post before the opposing team can hit one of the wickets with the retrieved ball. If the batsman can prevent that from happening, he is rewarded with a run. If a hitter drives the ball to the edge of the field, he scores four runs and if it goes beyond the boundary without touching the ground – a "home run," so to speak – six runs are scored.

Each team has two bowlers, each of whom tosses an "over" of six balls before taking a turn at fielding, while his mate displays his skills at such things as throwing breaking balls, which cricket fans call "googlies." A batsman is retired if a fielder catches a fly ball and he's out if the ball hits his leg and would have hit the wicket if his leg hadn't been there, at which time the "leg before wicket" rule comes into play. This isn't football, after all. It obviously isn't baseball, either. And if you think it might be a fast-paced, action-packed game, you're wrong. Cricket fans traditionally spend as much time at the local pub as in the hot sun and they rarely come back to the edge of the "pitch," as the territory between the wickets is called, with the feeling of having missed much. Play continues until ten of the eleven players are out and the other side gets its innings at bat. But a cricket match doesn't go on forever, it just seems that way. Most are limited to one day, and if all the innings haven't been played by sundown, the match is declared a draw. Professional matches are limited to three days and the really big international competitions, appropriately called "tests," go on for five. The game is sometimes speeded up by a rule that allows a team with a substantial lead to declare its innings over and concentrate on "dismissing" opposing batsmen. Weatherwise captains often "declare" at the first sign of rain, giving their opponents the disadvantage of playing on wet grass, the dreaded "sticky wicket."

The rules of cricket have hardly changed since the early

eighteenth century, and the taverns whose profits are often enhanced by those rules have been on the scene even longer. The signs that identify many of them are as good as a guidebook for clues to local history and regional pride. The Bat and Ball at Hambledon claims to be the one that hosted the spectators at the very first cricket game, for instance. Many are named for kings and princes who sampled their hospitality, others note the return of crusaders with paintings of Saracens' heads. A spread eagle symbolizes that German wines were once available under the sign, and Bag O'Nails reflects the British aversion to foreign-sounding words like bacchanals even though they don't mind adopting such foreign pursuits. During the Roman occupation, a sprig of ivy, the symbol of their god Bacchus, usually marked places where wine was sold, but creative publicans began dotting the countryside with places called Bird-in-Hand, which everyone knew was worth at least double the pleasure that could be found under any old ivy bush.

Most pubs, though independently owned, carry the name of the brewery that supplies them. Those not tied to a particular supplier announce the fact by calling themselves "Free Houses." But until recently neither was free to stay open all the livelong day, though some designated as "Off Licence" could sell liquor to take away for off-hours consumption. It was thought un-British, vaguely immoral and, in fact, illegal to belly up to a bar in the early morning, mid-afternoon or late evening. England was the only country on earth where for over seventy years closing time came twice in twenty-four hours as sure as the tides that flood and drain her harbors. The custom dated back to World War I, when the government wanted to reassure the Tommies at the front that the folks back home weren't spending the whole day drinking when there were guns and artillery shells to be made. Parliament has now passed a law allowing pubs to open from eleven to eleven. At closing time in some places, towels are ceremoniously hung over the beer pumps, the lights turned out and the doors are opened to cool enthusiasm for that one last drink. At one time the law was quite specific that when the hands of the clock reached the appointed hour, glasses, no matter how full, were not to be touched by any hands except those of the landlord. Parliament wrestled with the problem, which was causing many a pint to be quaffed in a matter of seconds, and debated allowing fifteen minutes to consume unfinished drinks. The discussion was finally settled in a typically British compromise – ten minutes of drink-up time. But not a second more, mind you.

Tourists accustomed to late afternoon cocktail hours used to find England's licensing laws less than quaint, but the natives themselves still have something better to do in the late afternoon hours. It's tea time.

The Boston Teaparty notwithstanding, the English passion for tea didn't begin to become a part of the national character until about the time the unpleasantness in America came to an end. Even after 1800, when all England had accepted tea as "the cups that cheer but not inebriate," gin was still the national drink, after good strong ale, and in the 1870s per capita annual consumption of the stuff reached 1.3 gallons, washed down with 34.4 gallons of beer and ale for every man, woman and child in the country. But the Victorians, even though they couldn't help agreeing with the working class that gin was "the quickest way out of Manchester," made tea not only fashionable, but an indispensable part of English life.

Mrs. Isabella Beeton, who was the arbiter of household management in those days, suggested that afternoon tea was an outgrowth of weekly "at homes" in the upperclass homes of earlier eras. Her menu suggestions included bread and butter, cake and fresh fruit. The occasion demanded entertainment by the guests themselves in the form of a musical offering or a recitation. But she cautioned that the selections should be short because guests usually came to tea "to meet their friends and have a chat," which may also be the reason why servants, once having set the tea and snacks in place, were required to leave the room and leave the pouring to the hostess or a selected guest. It left the ladies free to let the discussion go anywhere it might lead, even in the direction of the servant problem.

Family teas were an everyday occurrence in the 1880s if Mrs. Beeton is to be believed. The fare expanded to include finger sandwiches, sardines and potted meats as well as other "eminently feminine" offerings. The idea was especially popular, she said, because "the young folks are never excluded by reason of age as they would be at a late dinner." Even more popular among the young, she said, was high tea, "which will not interfere with tennis, boating or other amusements, and but little formality is needed." These days, fancy hotels and tea rooms in every part of the country advertize high tea that includes tiny sandwiches, a pastry or two and scones with preserves and clotted cream served with great formality at high prices. But as a piece of Victoriana, it is more like an "at home," even including a harpist providing soft background music. As Mrs. Beeton described it, high tea usually included "one or two small hot dishes, cold chicken, or game, tongue or ham, salad, cakes of various kinds, sometimes cold fruit tarts with cream or custard and fresh fruit." She said it should be somewhat like a cross between a first-rate luncheon and an early supper, and even suggested that the tea itself should be relegated to the sideboard and "wine only, in the way of drink put upon the table."

But in modern England, tea is never relegated to the sideboard. For people in every walk of life it is the best-loved beverage, and it isn't uncommon for an Englishman, conservative in every other way, to wolf down a dozen cups a day, possibly three of them before getting out of bed in the morning. Cultures that take tea less seriously take it with a slice of lemon; Americans have even been known to add ice cubes to it and millions around the world are so casual about it that they think making a cup of tea involves nothing more than dropping a little bag into a cup of boiling water. But in most English households, such things will never do. A proper cup of tea needs to be strong, piping hot, freshly brewed and generously laced with milk and sugar. Though the teapot may be filled and refilled a dozen times a day, it is carefully washed and dried after each use. Before the tea is carefully measured into it, one spoonful for each cup and another for the pot, it is warmed with hot water and emptied because cold china is said to ruin the leaves. The water in the kettle, meanwhile, has been brought to a full boil and when all is ready, the pot is carried to the kettle rather than the other way around so that the temperature won't drop even a fraction of a degree and spoil the flavor. The instant the pot is full, it is stirred quickly, the top put into place and it is put aside under a tea cozy to steep for a couple of minutes. The cups are then partially filled with milk, and when the tea itself has been added, the concoction is rounded off with a generous amount of sugar. But before it can be drunk, the teapot is taken back to the kettle to be refilled with boiling water and placed under the cozy again in readiness for a second cup. Any variation in this painstaking ritual is unthinkable. Any more satisfying cup of tea is unknown.

Foreigners who don't understand the ways of the English often regard them as quaint and charming, but they are much more than that. And if their empire has gone with the wind, they haven't wasted much time mourning its passing. As one of their poetic philosophers pointed out, they have always had more admiration for things like small cottages, small gardens, small women and small dogs, and most of all, for their small island, which one of its favorite sons once called "This land of such dear souls, this dear, dear land."

Facing page: Land's End, the westernmost point in England, at the end of the Penwith Peninsula in Cornwall.

Above left: Longships Lighthouse beyond Land's End, Cornwall, and (above) Polperro, a village as pretty and as well preserved as St. Ives (facing page top and below). Despite intensive commercialization, both of these famous Cornish villages have retained their lime-washed houses and narrow streets. St. Ives was once a busy fishing port which grew up around a small chapel built by Saint Ia in the sixth century. Today, however, most, if not all, of the fishing is done by holiday-makers. Below left: the huge granite rocks near Newquay, Cornwall, which, according to legend, are the stepping stones of the giant Beduthan. Left: green sward cloaks the cliffs down to the sea beside Cornwall's Mevagissy harbor and (facing page bottom) the sparkling white houses of East Looe, seen from West Looe, in Cornwall, cluster in tiers by the busy harborside.

Above: Teignmouth, reputedly Devon's oldest seaside town – even in 1340 the port was large enough to merit being attacked by the French. By 1818, when Keats corrected the proofs of one of his poems while staying at the resort, Teignmouth was well established. Built on the Teign estuary, the town boasts a pier, fine sand beaches and excellent golfing. Left: Salcombe, Devon, one of the most beautifully situated seaside towns in England. Until the late nineteenth century the main business here was building schooners. Today this town, the most southerly in Devon, welcomes visitors from all over the world. Top right: the Valley of the Rocks near Lynton, north Devon, and (above right) Jacob's Ladder on the Esplanade in Sidmouth, which is situated in a gap in east Devon's superb red cliffs. Right: Ilfracombe, which, like most of the larger West Country resorts, became popular during the Napoleonic Wars. Then Europe was a forbidding place for English holidaymakers; the war on the Continent obliged them to look for alternative resorts in their own country and Ilfracombe benefited. Situated on the north coast between hills and cliffs, the town was no more than a fishing village until the fourteenth century, when it grew into a sizeable trading port. Today its square harbor is attractive, being full of small craft and surrounded by mostly Victorian buildings. The bird reserve of Lundy lies offshore and boat trips to the island can be taken from Ilfracombe, as can cruises along the coast and across to Wales.

Left: the ruins of thirteenth-century Glastonbury Abbey, which was built on the site of the little wattle-and-daub church Joseph of Arimathea was reputed to have built here. Joseph is credited with making the first conversions to Christianity in Britain and the site is still a place of pilgrimage. Legend claims that on a nearby hill he thrust his staff into the ground and it took root to produce the Glastonbury thorn tree. The tree was destroyed in the Civil War, but a winter-flowering thorn in the abbey grounds is believed to have grown from a cutting. King Arthur and Queen Guinevere are thought to be buried in the abbey. Set in glorious countryside – typically English in appearance – Wells (below), the county town of Somerset, is dominated by its medieval cathedral (below left). Begun in 1180, this cathedral is considered to be one of the finest of its kind in the country, boasting a superb fan-vaulted ceiling in the Chapter House, a beautiful Lady Chapel dating from the fourteenth century and an equally impressive nave. The cathedral's west front is the pride of Somerset. It is said that in the seventeenth-century courtyard of Wells' Crown public house, William Penn preached to an audience of 2,000 and was arrested. Right: Widecombe-in-the-Moor, which is set high on Dartmoor in Devon. Widecombe's splendid church was hit by lightning during a service in 1638, killing four people and injuring over sixty. The story is related inside the church, and goes on to claim that a survivor recalled seeing a mysterious traveler in the village who had accidentally exposed a cloven hoof ….

Below: smooth water gives a perfect reflection of elegant Pulteney Bridge in Bath, Somerset, designed in 1777 by Robert Adams for William Pulteney, the first earl of Bath. First known for its springs, Bath came to prominence in the ninth century through its abbey, which was used for the coronation of Edward, the first king of England – the ceremony used then became the basis for all future coronation services. The present building (facing page bottom) was the work of Oliver King, a fifteenth-century Bishop of Bath and Wells. Facing page top: Somerset's Clifton Suspension Bridge.

17

Above: Bibury, typical of the quaint villages built of local stone in the Cotswolds, West Midlands. This village was considered the loveliest in England by the Victorian craftsman William Morris. Left: a fine garden in Dursley and (below) Buckland cottages, both Gloucestershire villages that have changed little since they were built. Facing page: (bottom) Hidcote Manor Garden, a twentieth-century garden near Chipping Campden, and (top) Naunton village, both in Gloucestershire.

Facing page: Herefordshire thatched cottages, whose style can be seen in many parts of the country; Holland House (below right) in Cropthorne, Worcestershire, is not dissimilar in appearance. Above: twelfth-century All Saints' Church and (below) the superb sixteenth-century bell tower, both in Evesham (right), Worcestershire. Above right: the mill and the abbey tower in Tewkesbury, a Gloucestershire town with a wealth of old houses and timbered inns.

Above: the church at Affpuddle in Dorset, the county where Thomas Hardy was born and the setting for most of his novels. Left: Hardy's cottage, Higher Bockhampton, and (below) Salisbury Cathedral, Wiltshire, possibly the loveliest in England. Facing page: (top) Stonehenge on Salisbury Plain, Wiltshire, and (bottom) Corfe Castle, Dorset, where King Edward was murdered in 978.

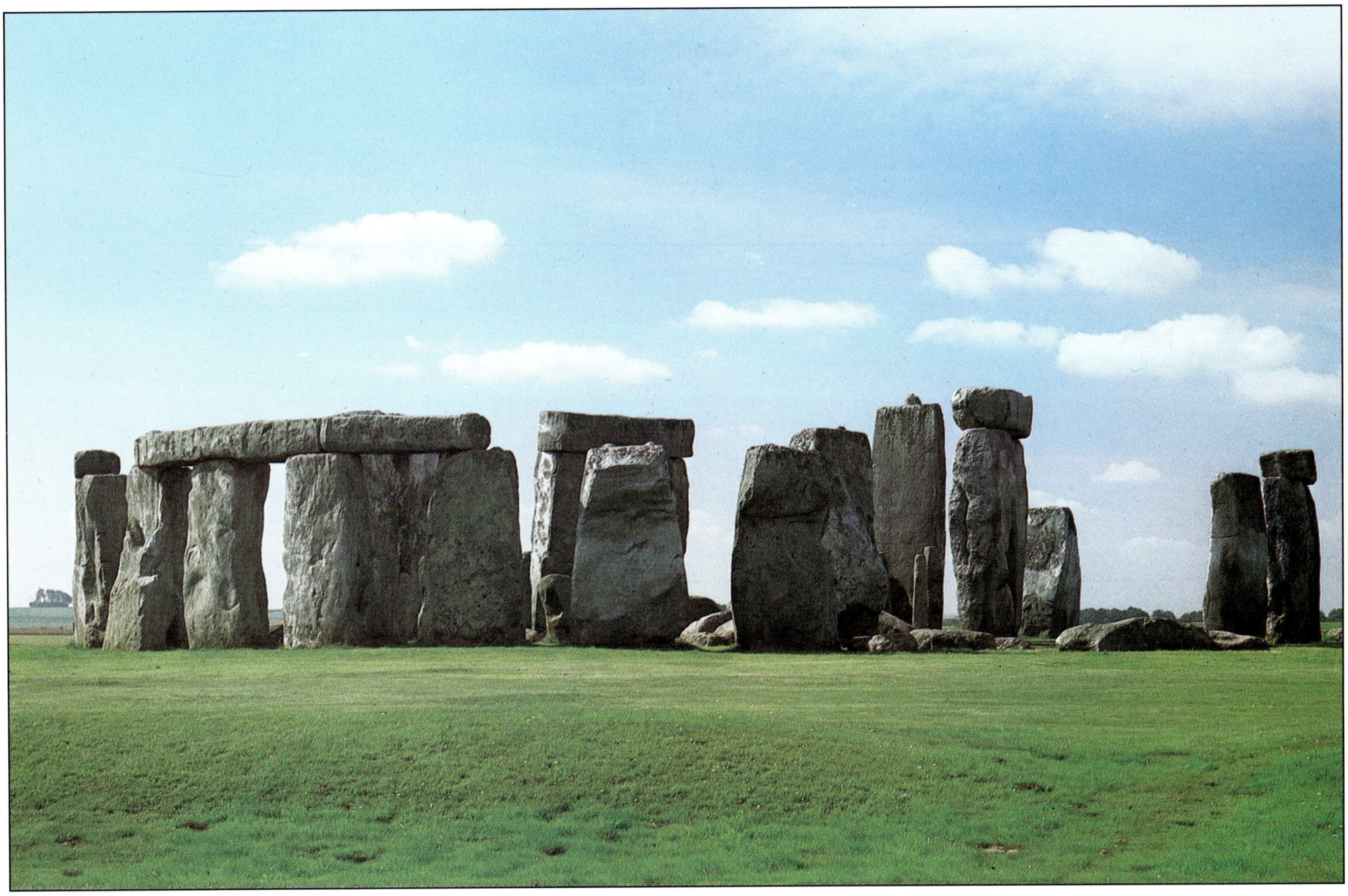

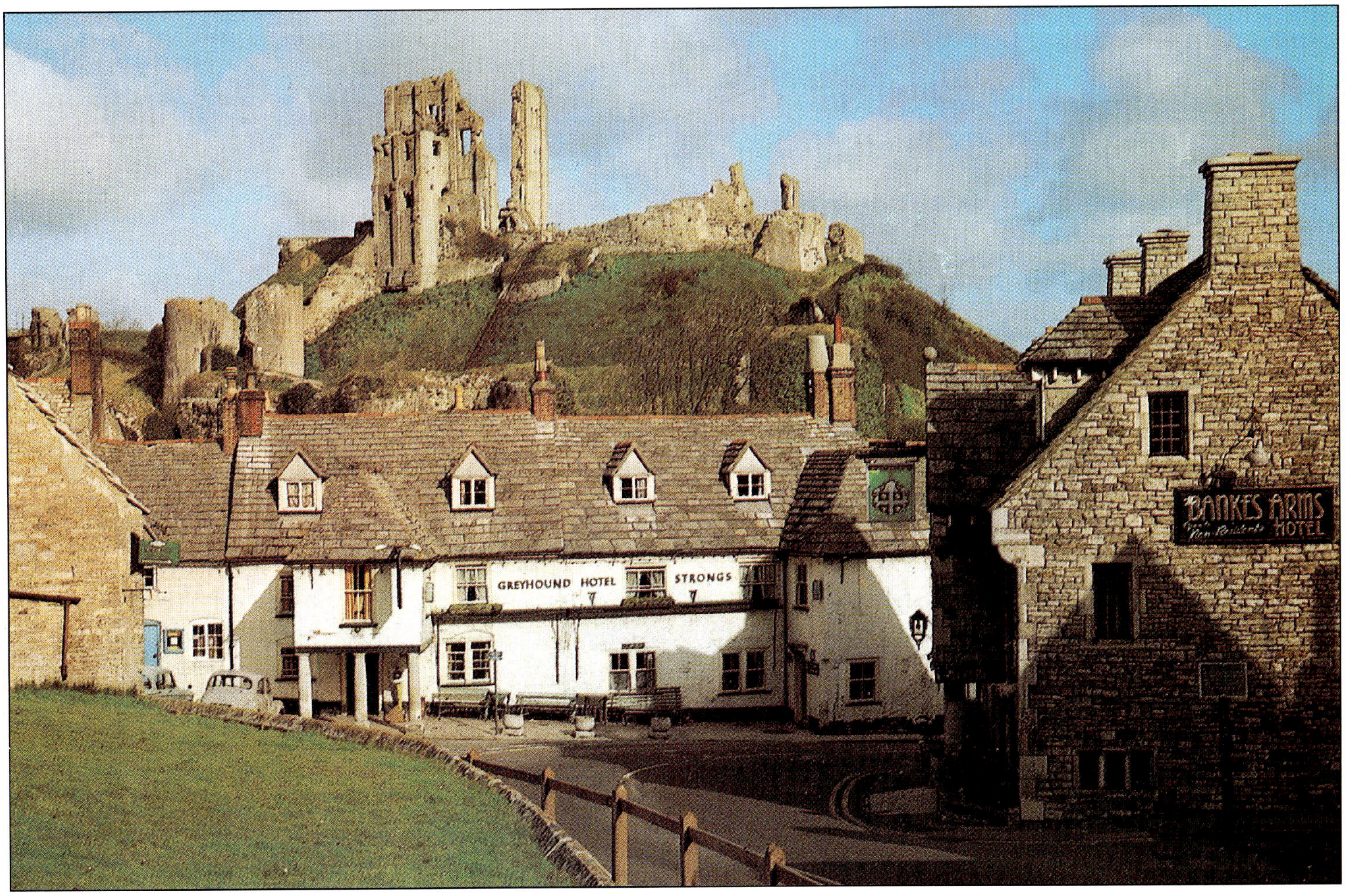
GREYHOUND HOTEL
STRONGS
BANKES ARMS
HOTEL

Left: the limestone arch known as Durdle Dor, near Lulworth Cove on the Dorset coast. It is likely that in time the top of the arch will be so eroded by waves that it will drop into the sea, leaving a pillar similar to others found along this coast, such as those at Old Harry Rocks (below) near the resort town of Swanage (right). Below right: Wareham, Dorset, which is situated on a ridge between the rivers Frome and Piddle. Once an important Anglo-Saxon river port, today Wareham is largely Georgian in character as its older buildings were destroyed in a great fire in 1762. Its church, St. Martin's, dates from the eleventh century and is the oldest extant church in the county. It contains an effigy of T. E. Lawrence – Lawrence of Arabia – who died not far from the town. Bottom right: Bournemouth, Hampshire, at the height of the summer season. Bournemouth, one of the best south coast resorts, has few buildings dating back more than a 120 years – in the early nineteenth century most of the land was still wild moorland. Today the town can boast a first-class symphony orchestra, a pier, a pavilion and a theater – facilities to match those of the queen of the south coast resorts, Brighton.

Facing page top: Bucklers Hard, a tiny village on the Beaulieu River, once a shipbuilding center which supplied forty of Nelson's ships for the Napoleonic War. Facing page bottom: the yacht marina, Lymington, where Quay Hill runs down to the Lymington River. Below: Georgian houses in the town's Nelson Place. Above: busy Portsmouth Harbor, beyond which lies the Isle of Wight.

Facing page top: the South Downs near Lewes (above), the county town of East Sussex, where Thomas Paine, the revolutionary, started to write pamphlets while he was an excise officer. Facing page bottom: the Seven Sisters, the chalk cliffs that stretch from Brighton to Eastbourne, where 600-foot-high Beachy Head (below) forms a sheer rock face against the sea. Above right: Arundel Castle in Sussex, often described as a smaller edition of Windsor Castle, the Berkshire residence of the sovereign. Right: Bodiam Castle, Winchelsea, Sussex, which stands surrounded by a lake-like moat and almost seems to float. Built in 1385, although the castle looks complete externally, closer investigation proves it to be a well-preserved ruin. The castle was besieged during the Civil War and has not been inhabited since. It was rescued from decay by Lord Curzon of Kedleston and today it is cared for by the National Trust. Below right: the Old Mill, Fittleworth, Sussex.

Above left: the fifteenth-century Mermaid Inn in Rye, Sussex, which, like Hastings (above), was one of the original Cinque Ports, though today it lies two miles inland from the receding sea on the River Rother. In the Middle Ages, the Cinque Ports were charged with the duty of providing ships in time of war. Left: Eastbourne's beach and pier. This Sussex town claims the most hours of sunshine of all the south coast resorts – more even than its great rival, Brighton, where shops in the Lanes (below) are a distraction even in the rain. Below left: the fifteenth-century White Horse Inn in the Kent village of Chilham, considered to be one of the least spoilt villages in a country full of unspoilt places, such as Farmingham (facing page top) and Ightham (facing page bottom), the setting of Ightham Mote, one of the last moated manor houses in England.

Right: the curious towered tithe barn that lies opposite the ancient church at Buckland, a village lying between Dorking and Reigate in Surrey. Below: Aylesford on the River Medway, a village that lies only three miles from the county town of Kent, Maidstone, and yet which retains an air of rural peace and a strong sense of its own identity. It boasts a number of old houses and a restored medieval bridge across the Medway. On the outskirts of the village lies a Carmelite friary. The original monastery was dissolved by Henry VIII, but Carmelites were able to re-establish it fifty years ago and although many of the buildings had been pulled down or allowed to decay over the intervening four hundred years, they were able to restore much of the medieval fabric, in particular the fifteenth-century Pilgrims' Hall. Aylesford was on the pilgrim route to Kent's Canterbury Cathedral, a place of pilgrimage after the martyrdom of Thomas à Becket. Facing page: white irises bloom in early summer beside oast houses that have been converted into homes outside Tonbridge, Kent. Oast houses were built on farms to contain kilns used in the drying of the hops grown in Kent for beer-making – during the hop harvest in September, their furnaces would remain alight day and night and tending them was one of the most important jobs on the farm. Since hops are no longer grown in vast quantities, today many oast houses lie unused, but their distinctive conical brick roofs and white cowls remain all over the county. Recognizable for miles, they are still a typical feature of the Kent landscape.

Left: the Norman church in Alfold, Surrey. The village also boasts old stocks and a whipping post, medieval methods of punishment. Above: Elizabethan houses in central Godalming, a Surrey town on the River Wey. Though it is hardly famous, Godalming has hosted two foreign kings during its long history. In its appropriately-named Kings Arms hotel, two Russian tzars were entertained: Peter the Great in 1689 and Alexander I in 1816. Remaining pictures: Surrey cottages, blossom and creeper clad.

Facing page top: Buckingham Palace, the London residence of the reigning sovereign. George III bought it as a dower house for Queen Charlotte in 1761 and it has been owned by the Royal Family ever since. Facing page bottom: Nelson's Column in Trafalgar Square, which marks the English victory over Napoleon's navy at Trafalgar in 1805. Above: Big Ben clock tower, part of the Palace of Westminster. The clock is one of the most famous sights of the city – Londoners regularly set their watches by it. The clock's chimes are heard on the hour, the notes of which accompany a phrase in Handel's Messiah: "All through this hour Lord be my Guide/ And by Thy Power no foot shall slide."

Facing page: St. Paul's Cathedral, the fifth cathedral to be built on this site, the first being dedicated in 604. Above: one of the four clock faces of Big Ben, and (above right) the Tower of London, the most perfect medieval fortress in England, built by William the Conqueror shortly after the Norman Conquest to awe the people into submission. It is still awe-inspiring today. Tower Bridge (right), close by, was built in the Gothic style in the 1890s. London's best-known bridge, it has an opening span of 200 feet. Below right: the world-famous Houses of Parliament on the banks of the River Thames and (below) reflections of a modern sculpture in London's new Docklands development.

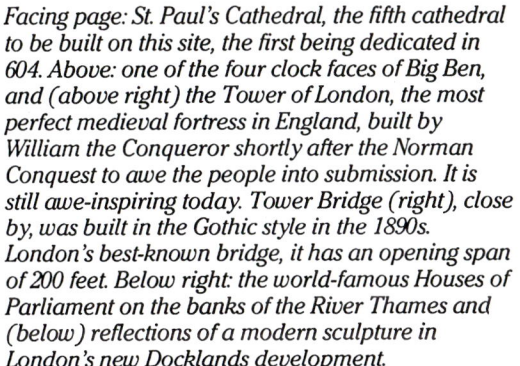

Above: the immaculately designed gardens of Hampton Court Palace, near Richmond, Surrey, the favorite country home of Henry VIII. Like the villages of Molesey (left) and Abingdon (below) in Oxfordshire, it lies beside the River Thames, once an important transportation route. Windsor Castle (facing page top) was also served by this mighty waterway. The town of Windsor (facing page bottom) has retained its historical charm.

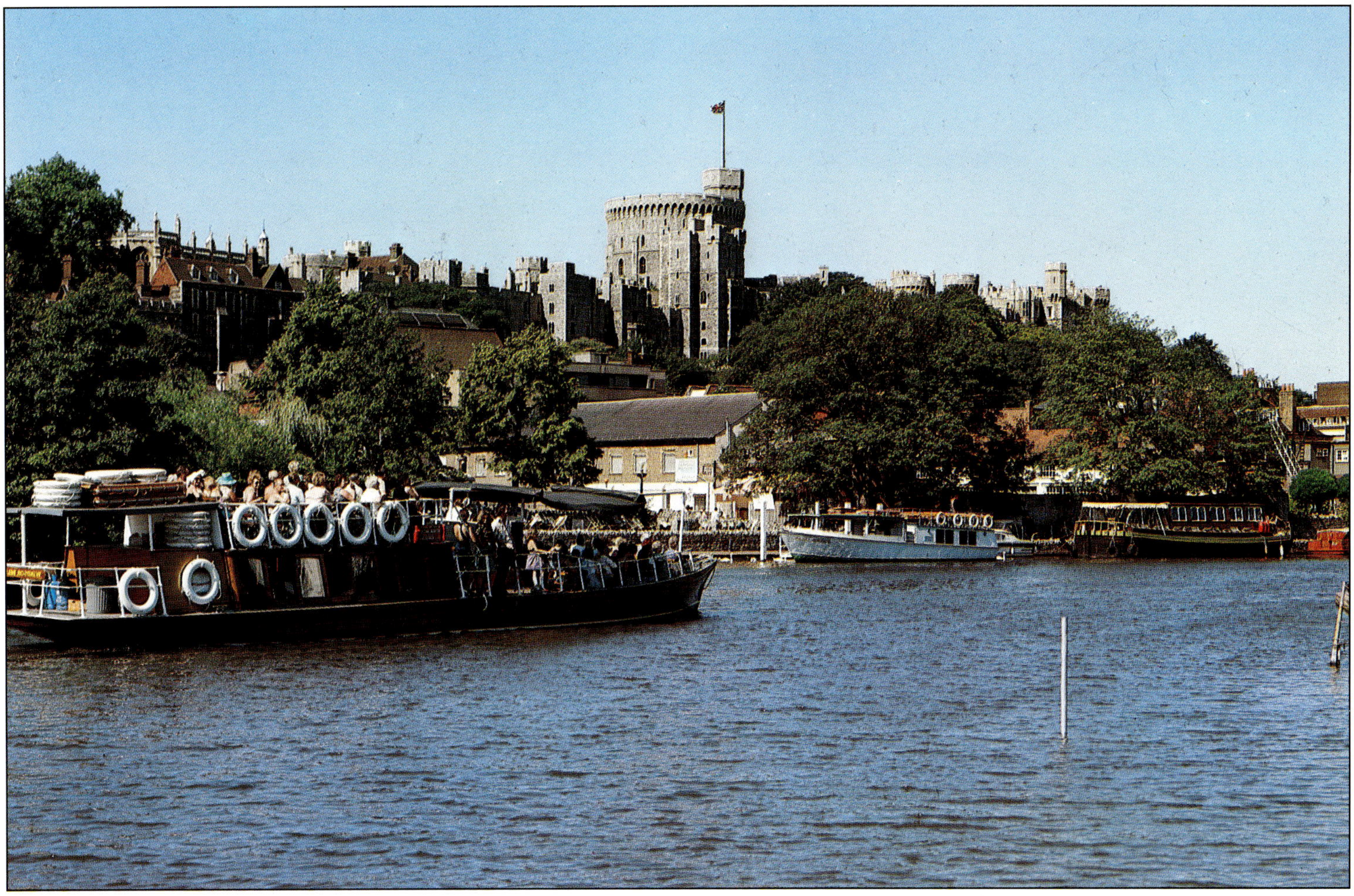

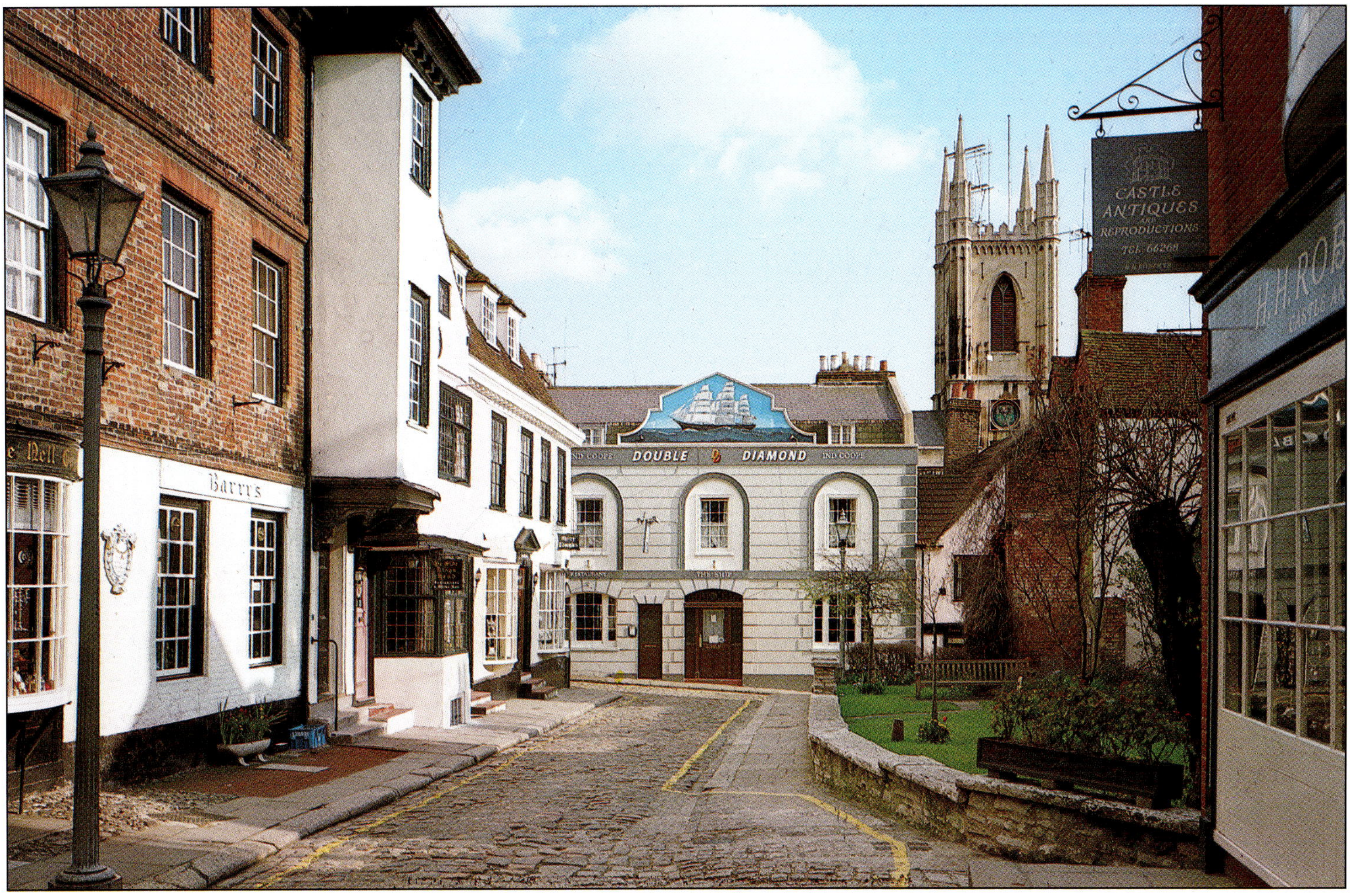

DOUBLE DIAMOND
Barry's
CASTLE ANTIQUES AND REPRODUCTIONS TEL. 66268

Some of the oldest in the world, the colleges of Oxford University (these pages) are also some of the most beautiful. Facing page: (top) Nuffield College, a graduate college founded in 1937, and (bottom) St. John's College, founded in 1555. Below: St. Edmund Hall, a unique survival of the early residential societies for undergraduates, was founded in 1220 and given full college status this century. Above and right: one of the best known "dreaming spires," Magdalen College bell tower.

Suffolk villages such as Sapiston (above) and Cavendish (left) have been the inspiration of many, but Suffolk is above all Constable country. John Constable, the acclaimed eighteenth-century landscape artist, was born in the county in 1776. The artist went to school in Lavenham (facing page), the most resplendent of Suffolk wool towns with a wealth of fine medieval timber houses. The market square is dominated by the Guildhall (above left) which at various times has been a prison, a workhouse and an almshouse. The original Wool Hall has been incorporated in the Swan Hotel (below left). Kersey (below), set in a steep-sided valley, is one of Suffolk's prettiest villages. Here a street of dark-timbered houses runs through a water-splash where ducks still take precedence over cars. An interesting bygone is the stallion's tail hanging from the eaves of a local veterinary surgeon's house. The village church, St. Mary's, lies on a hill overlooking Kersey and is mentioned in the Domesday Book.

46

Facing page top: the romantic ruins of the Cluniac Priory in Castle Acre. The priory was founded in 1090 for a Benedictine order established in the previous century. Its exceptional remains include fine Norman arcading and a Tudor gatehouse. Facing page bottom: Blickling Hall, Norfolk, one of the country's greatest showpieces, a superb Jacobean house built between 1616 and 1627 for Sir Henry Hobart. It was later owned by the Boleyn family – it is believed that Anne Boleyn was born in an earlier house on the site. Right: Burghley House, near Stamford, Cambridgeshire, an Elizabethan mansion that stands in a great park where the Burghley horse trials are held every September. Completed in 1589 by Elizabeth I's Lord High Treasurer, William Cecil, the first Lord Burghley, the house was built on the site of a monastery. One of the largest mansions of its kind in the country, the house contains over 700 works of art, and is particularly famous for its Heaven Room, where the wall and ceiling paintings by Verrio are considered masterpieces. Its magnificent walled park was designed by Capability Brown, who included an orangery, a lake and a superb rose garden in his plans. Burghley has been the home of the Cecils and Exeters for 400 years. Below: the Broadland village known as Potter Heigham on the River Thurne in Norfolk. A large number of holidaymakers visit this yachting center by both road and water.

Cambridge is recognized throughout Europe as one of its most beautiful cities. Much of the glory of its architecture is found in its university colleges. Above left: Clare College, founded as University Hall in 1326 to be refounded by Elizabeth de Burgh of Clare, hence its current name, twenty years later. Left: fall sunshine highlights Kings College Chapel, possibly the finest Gothic building in Britain. Its pale gold stone interior, especially its fan-vaulted ceiling, is breathtaking in its artistry. Below: a colorful herbaceous border outside Trinity Hall, which was founded in 1350 and is not to be confused with the separate establishment of Trinity College (above and facing page bottom), founded in 1336 as King's Hall and refounded in 1546 by Henry VIII as Trinity College. Facing page top: the immaculate courtyard of Christ's College and (below left) Ely Cathedral.

Facing page: Compton Wynyates, a Tudor manor house beautifully set in a hollow of hills in the heart of Warwickshire. Built from pink brick, mellow stone and weathered wood, the house is full of secret passages, sliding panels and hidden rooms. It is believed that it contains nearly a hundred rooms and over 300 windows. Wynyates is Old English for windy valley. Equally interesting is Warwickshire's Packwood House (right and below), also an example of Tudor architecture. Its yew tree walk is famous – the trees are grouped to represent Christ preaching to his followers in the Sermon on the Mount. Above: Barton on the Heath, Warwickshire.

Above: Welford-upon-Avon, which lies south of Stratford-upon-Avon (left), the Warwickshire town famous as the birthplace of perhaps the world's greatest playwright, William Shakespeare. Below: Holy Trinity Church, where Shakespeare rests, close to the River Avon in Stratford. Facing page: Anne Hathaway's charming cottage. Anne was Shakespeare's wife and some years his senior.

Facing page: Chester Cathedral. On this site a church or minster was founded in the tenth century to hold the body of St. Werburgh. In 1092, the Earl of Chester made it into an abbey for Benedictine monks and for five centuries this monastery was powerful and owned much land in the region. After the Dissolution the abbey became a cathedral. The nave, although begun in the fourteenth century, was not finished until the sixteenth. Much of the architecture in Chester (below), the county town of Cheshire, is medieval in appearance, and black-and-white buildings, both medieval and Victorian, are a definite feature. The only city in England to have preserved its city walls in their entirety, it is possible to take a two-mile circular walk right around Chester and experience superb views of the town and the surrounding countryside along the way. Once the tower at the northwest corner of the wall stood in water – Chester was an important port in the thirteenth and fourteenth centuries – but then the River Dee silted up, which subsequently choked the trade between the city and Ireland and parts of the Continent. Right: Little Moreton Hall, unquestionably the finest example of black-and-white half-timbered architecture in England. This sixteenth-century moated manor house boasts a chapel, a great hall and a knot garden. A rather obvious secret room behind the chimney breast was designed to be discovered without too much trouble, in the hope that the family's enemies would abandon the search for any other secret places. All the while, far below the moat, at the end of a tortuous underground passage, there remained a tiny cell, which served as the real hiding place.

Above: the Royal Liver Building and its famous "Liver birds" in Liverpool, one of England's largest ports. The city's Roman Catholic Metropolitan Cathedral (left) is of an avant garde design. Below and facing page top: Blackpool Tower, which boasts a splendid ballroom (facing page bottom).

The Lake District (these pages) in Cumbria, northwest England, is an area of natural beauty only some thirty miles across. Much of it lies in the Lake District National Park, which was established in 1951 to preserve these world-famous landscapes. For several centuries the peaks and lakes here have been a mecca for poets, artists and visitors from all round the globe – indeed, nowhere else in rural England is so closely associated with literature. Coleridge and Wordsworth are the most famous Lakeland writers; Wordsworth lived for nine years in Dove Cottage in the village of Grasmere (above) which takes its name from the lake (right). The cottage became a meeting place for such famous literary figures as Southey and de Quincey, as well as Coleridge. Shelley and Sir Walter Scott also spent time here, gaining inspiration from the majesty of the land. Bowness lies on Lake Windermere (left), the largest lake in England, set at the center of the Lake District. The town is the headquarters of the Royal Windermere Yacht Club, but there are facilities here for hiring all manner of craft beside yachts, from rowing boats to high-powered launches. At ten-and-a-half-miles long, this great lake has been a highway for the transport of goods for centuries. Above left: Tarn Hows in the Lake District, one of its loveliest beauty spots.

Top left: dry-stone walls above the Yorkshire village of Malham, where the products of a stony land have been put to good use – as they have in the walls of North Yorkshire villages such as Muker (above), a remote hamlet in Upper Swaledale. Above left: the Shambles, a medieval street in York. York Minster is the largest medieval church in northern Europe and holds England's greatest concentration of medieval stained glass. The city has also retained its impressive medieval city walls (left), reminiscent of the time when York was England's second city, a great religious and commercial center based upon the wool trade. Right: the port of Whitby, North Yorkshire, which lies on the mouth of the River Esk. The house of the famous English explorer Captain Cook can be viewed here, as can the ruins of a Benedictine monastery and church high on a cliff beside the sea. More jet, or fossilized wood, is found in the Whitby area than anywhere else in Britain. Used for jewellery, this stone was particularly popular with the Victorians, who used it for mourning brooches. In 1873 over 200 workshops thrived here.

Durham Cathedral (facing page top), one of the most dramatically situated cathedrals in the country, was begun in 1093 by the Norman bishop, William of Calais. It stands on a seventy-foot-high rock surrounded on three sides by the River Wear. Older even than Durham is the enormous stone edifice of Bamburgh Castle (above) in Northumberland – it was founded in 547 by King Ida. Facing page bottom: the ruins of St. Mary's in York and (right) the stark remains of Whitby Abbey beside the North Sea in North Yorkshire. Also set above this sea is the sixteenth-century castle of Lindisfarne (above right), Northumberland. Bolton Abbey (below), in North Yorkshire, has been much loved by painters – the Victorian artist Landseer made it famous with a work entitled Bolton Abbey in Olden Time, *and its setting is indeed romantic. However it is Rievaulx Abbey (below right) that is probably the most beautifully situated of all the monastic ruins in North Yorkshire – even Turner painted this site. Overleaf: swiftly passing clouds cast dark shadows over the hills on a summer's day near Hawes in Wensleydale, North Yorkshire. The little village of Hawes lies on the River Ure between two of England's highest passes and near the 850-foot-high head of Wensleydale.*

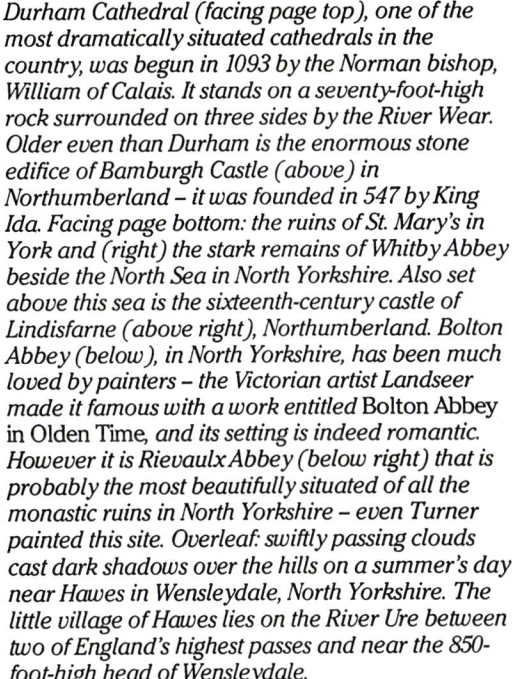